I0171773

Spectral Realms

No. 24 ‡ Winter 2026

Edited by S. T. Joshi

The spectral realms that thou canst see
With eyes veil'd from the world and me.

H. P. LOVECRAFT, "To a Dreamer"

SPECTRAL REALMS is published twice a year by Hippocampus Press,
P.O. Box 641, New York, NY 10156 (www.hippocampuspress.com).
Copyright © 2026 by Hippocampus Press.
All works are copyright © 2026 by their respective authors.
Cover art: *Polar Aurora Borealis* by M. Rapine (c. 1872), after Silbermann
and Bévalet, 1839. Cover design by Daniel V. Sauer
Hippocampus Press logo by Anastasia Damianakos.

ISBN 978-1-61498-491-7   ISSN 2333-4215

Contents

Poems 5

Yuggoth at the Rim / Ann K. Schwader 7

Testimony of a Shade / Scott J. Couturier.............................. 8

Only Stubborn Souls Will Succeed / Andrew White 10

Hell Radio / F. J. Bergmann.. 11

the erlking / Lee Clark Zumpe 12

His Implacable Regard / David C. Kopaska-Merkel...................... 13

There Were No More Words, Except Freedom / Maxwell I. Gold....14

A Song for Pan / Dmitri Akers 15

The Gargoyle's Cat / Lori R. Lopez 16

Leaf Encounter / Michael Rollins....................................... 18

The Red Fog / Wade German.. 20

Underlying Cause / John Shirley 21

Red Thoughts / Simon MacCulloch....................................... 22

Of Xenomorphs in the Black Abyss / Manuel Pérez-Campos............ 23

A Rare Trait in Rabbits and Mice / Steven Withrow........................ 24

Briar Rose / DJ Tyrer.. 27

After the Burning / Jacqueline West 28

Trapdoor Beneath the Feet of the Hangèd Man / Kendall Evans 30

Serpentine Stitch (Decaying Seams) / Eli Alemán.......................... 32

Immortal Bird / David Barker.. 35

The River Beneath the Floor / Flavia Pierret............................ 36

The Baleen Clock / Joshua Green 37

Dracacyn / Adam Bolivar 38

Spirit Sleuth / A. J. Dalton 40

The Ghosts That I See Are All My Own / Darrell Schweitzer............ 43

The Best Employee / Norbert Góra 44

a ubiquitous silence / Lee Clark Zumpe 46

Echoes in the Shade / Ngo Binh Anh Khoa.............................. 47

This Dread Glimpse / David McLachlan.................................. 48

Autumn's Crown / Scott J. Couturier 50

Apocalypse Kisses / Pixie Bruner 52

A (Familiar) Cosmic Gathering / Maxwell I. Gold........................ 56

Homecoming / Silvatiicus Riddle 58

Blinding / Nicholas De Marino 59

Extinction / Michael Potts 60

Tribe / Allan Rozinski 61

Invasion from the Worst of All Possible Worlds / Manuel Pérez-
    Campos 64

Theobald Vesselldoom: An Albino Four-Leaf Clover /
    Wade German 66

Her Ways / Jay Hardy 70

Honorary God / Jay Sturner 72

Baba Yaga / Christian Dickinson 73

The Diver / Alper Ghuchlu 74

After Perrault / Geoffrey Reiter 75

Breakout / Simon MacCulloch 76

Encounter / DJ Tyrer 78

Dormant Knoll / Steven Withrow 79

Dies Irae / Andrew Paul Wood 80

In Darkness / Adam Bolivar 81

The Face in the Night-Shrouded Window / John Shirley 82

To a Distant Star / Jason Ray Carney 84

Of Feathers and Vows / Eli Alemán 85

Dr. Frankenstein's Electro-Mechanical Monster / Kendall Evans 88

the wily moon / Lee Clark Zumpe 90

A Dread Cycle Renewed / David McLachlan 92

Fu-Pao, the Witch of the Northern Lights / Arukoya Tomais 93

k.t.u.l.k.h.u / Yuliia Vereta 97

Wicked Imp / Janice Klain 98

Surf's Up / Nicholas De Marino 99

Widowspins / Oliver Smith..100

On Golden Gate Bridge / Manuel Pérez-Campos 101

Bury Her / Scott J. Couturier 102

Classic Reprints...**103**

The Ghost / Mary Sharon 105

The Parrot / Alfred Noyes 106

Articles 109
   Clark Ashton Smith: Before *The Star-Treader* / S. T. Joshi 111
Reviews 119
   Firelight and Nightmuse: Two Poets Find Their Voices / Steven
      Withrow 121
   Lyrics and Shanties / S. T. Joshi 125
Notes on Contributors 127

Poems

Yuggoth at the Rim

Ann K. Schwader

Rejected from the first, it drifts apart
from other worlds, suspected yet unseen
by mundane science. Only at the heart
of dream it lingers, massive & serene
with primal mysteries. Its skies glow green
above spiked shadow cities windowless
yet tenanted. By what—or whom? Obscene
inhuman silhouettes take flight, transgress
all laws we thought we understood. Unless
our telescopes betray us, we may wait
in ignorance for centuries, oppressed
at unimagined distance. How this fate
deforms our lives & orbits, none can tell
save Providence's bard, who saw too well.

Testimony of a Shade

Scott J. Couturier

In that wide & rabid waste of desert
Came I on an ancient unopened tomb;
Long-buried in endlessly restless sands,
I did as my thievish nature demands
& entered its eld portal, wreathed by gloom.

Sour air within, unbearably arid;
A torch I bore to light my greedy way.
Strange sigils graven onto sandstone planes
Guided me towards a great king's remains,
By embalment kept from crumbling to clay.

Reaching a nether chamber, surely where
Pharaoh rested in death's deathless repose,
I found instead a wretched reptilian thing
Where should have lain a human being—
Talons a precious scepter clutching close.

After fear, avarice always prevails.
Atop this scepter a stone shone by glow
Of my brand's waning flame: a beryl
Worth wealth enough to risk baleful peril.
As I stared, my desire did only grow.

Doom, dark indweller of all mortal lusts:
At last reaching out, my robber's spoils to claim,
It was my own limbs which withered to dust.
Now even that tomb is gone, though I remain.

[Inspired by Lovecraft's "The Nameless City."]

Only Stubborn Souls Will Succeed

Andrew White

The road is full of trials
And strange obstacles in the way—
Only stubborn souls will succeed.

Past a field of carnivorous roses,
Where the ground shifts under your feet,
And the journey has just begun;

Through the forest of venomous pines,
With woodwives that tempt you to stay,
Toward blood-red skies beyond;

Across the river filled with bones,
Where undines pull from below,
Toward a shore with razor-sharp grass;

Up haunted hills to jagged peaks,
Where the stones themselves scream with hate,
The gates of Summerland await.

Hell Radio

F. J. Bergmann

Dim and dull idol in morning briskness,
all day long it squatted on the shelf
above the vegan cookbooks as fat flies crawled
through slow-moving bands of light. It waited,
ready to welcome us home each gloaming,
glowing ruby, waxing and waning, gloating
like a red moon. It was just what we needed
to beguile an idle hour. It needed no dial;
its horns were tuned to one station only, its power
always on. We never admitted listening to it,
but sometimes we would catch each other
on tiptoe, one ear pressed against its black
iron grille, whispering liturgical responses,
confessing a spectrum of interesting sins.

the erlking

Lee Clark Zumpe

something gliding through mystic darkness,
beneath a pantheon of mythologic dignitaries
consigned to parcels in prominent constellations;

something flitting in the soft moonlight,
negotiating the labyrinth of spreading branches
that swing and sway though the night is still;

something shadowing our benighted journey,
trailing us as we attempt the perilous trek
upon a mountainous, meandering road;

something grasping for its unwitting prey,
driven by an ancient, inescapable craving,
and executed with sophisticated malevolence.

something lingering amidst scattered debris,
down a steep embankment in a dark forest,
attended only by carrion eaters and kindred spirits.

His Implacable Regard

David C. Kopaska-Merkel

Cassilda is stuck on the lakeshore ride
at Carcosaland,
this creepy guy in a yellow suit
takes the empty seat beside her,
feels like he's oozing into her seat,
cold metal transformed to sludge,
but she has no place to go;
he pulls out a book,
her own name on the cover,
something drifts across the track,
reaches for her with attenuated fingers,
and something screams,
raising its long three-headed neck
from the muck,
ichor dripping from rubbery lips;
here we go again, she thinks,
and pinches herself,
to no avail.

Tickets punched,
the train squeals to a stop,
riders herded into the station,
the stench of the lake,
the wind from the abyss,
and the King,
icy finger lifting her chin.

There Were No More Words, Except Freedom

Maxwell I. Gold

Here at the end, there were no more words, only death and that endless dirge that came like the before-silence of a coming nuclear blast, followed by a radiant white oblivion. Ever present, but without consciousness and unknowingly hungry as if it devoured for no reason other than for the sake of itself. The Earth, the stars, and everything else bottomed out only when the very last possible atom gave way at the seemingly last moment at Entropy's irresistible pull like a breathless hope; pressed only for a moment to continue slightly longer as if a spool clinging to the last thread and continue forever as I realized there as truly no end to this depraved, cosmic lunacy.

And there were no words to explain that despicable, unthinkable blackness that swelled in the heat-frozen opaqueness that was infinity. No curse, no applicable hatred or indifferent ascribed to the irascible emptiness, here at the end except for the quiet, lonely inevitability draped in cold, physics and I knew then, I was truly free.

A Song for Pan

Dmitri Akers

Within the verdant sward that Pan commands,
There frolic satyrs, nymphs, and sprites that twirl—
To fifes and drums that wilderness demands,
As every magick creature joins that swirl
Of fur and scales, of sparkling wings and tails—
As screams may rise above the beasts that dance
With cloven hooves that stamp, as horrid wails
Awake the hornéd god to frig and prance
Along the blades of Arcadia's field;
He plucks the sprigs of *Spring* from *Winter's* clutch,
His yellow eyes—a goat's—may yearn to yield
The fertile soil that only spirits touch.
O Pan! Thy mouth has blown upon the fife
That sways the tree and gives the seed its life!

The Gargoyle's Cat

Lori R. Lopez

Out of a pitch-dark height dove a guardian
feather-clad, once perched in stone. Once
squatting atop the upper parapets, almost
among the clouds. Swooping in deft coils
like a great bat, circling down to bask below
a streetlamp's gaze—and spook a cat.

"Birdies are nice," Miss Dotty would say.
"They sing for us!" Her clever pet translated:
Don't kill those irksome flitting twits that tease
too much, gliding to taunt him from above.
Look don't touch! This birdy was bigger
than the lady, with a mad screeching howl.

Worse than any conniving flock of raucous
Crows! Fiercer than a diving Hawk or Owl.
And the woman no longer told him things.
Hard streets were home for a lean Tomcat,
blind in one eye after a nasty swipe. Glum,
shaggy, hugging shadows. Nerves taut . . .

Hunched and tension-fraught, a solitary soul.
Missing comforts of home; companionship.
Fitful, underfed, he yowled at the beastly
Chimera—insanely sculpted of a Lion's tail,

sturdy hindlegs. Tall ears and a Raptor Snout.
Eagle eyes and talons, plumed wings. *"Scat!"*

The Bird-Cat's nose swiveled, golden orb
pinpointing the small silhouette. Jojo archly
bristled and hissed—a ridged spine curved:
"Fly away!" with all the scorn a feline could
muster. "Come closer." The Gryphon smiled,
as best he might with a beak, and beckoned.

"Come, let's see." Curling a long wingtip . . .
The cat obliged, drawn by curiosity, head low,
dander high. A wary approach. The Gargoyle
plucked a quill and tapped a scar. The wound
disappeared, halting Jojo mid-snarl, touched
by kindness to purr, "I am the one who sees."

A wing unfurled. "Care to join me? The best
view in town." Side by side they bonded; soon
fast friends: a Gargoyle and his cat, peering
from the lofty Tower, 'neath a magickal Moon.

Leaf Encounter

Michael Rollins

"Won't you climb into my branches?" asked the grizzled tree;
"The day is dying quickly now, and there's only you and me."

"If I do, I'll never leave," the girl answered with a smile,
"but I don't mind standing out of reach, and talking for a while."

"For I have heard the many tales of boys and girls, like me,
 who disappeared into the leaves of a dark and ancient tree . . ."

"But I will tell you stories," replied the timeless one,
"of the magic I have witnessed since the Earth was young.

"I will tell you of Mer-people in their cities 'neath the sea;
 of dragons stealing Princesses; of knights who set them free;

"Of Faery-folk who ruled this land, defeating Orcs and Trolls,
 till Mankind stole their magic, and finally their souls."

Enchanted by his wondrous words, the child forgot her fear:
"Reach down your mighty boughs to me, for I would love to hear."

Then a shadow crossed the giant's face, of shame and regret.
"I may be monstrous now," he cried, "but I am not a monster yet!"

His great trunk trembled with heavy, rumbling sighs,
and tears of sap rolled down from the sadness in his eyes.

"You were wise to be wary, I was human once, you see:
a little boy, around your age, when I climbed into a tree . . ."

The Red Fog

Wade German

Across the moonlight-silvered sea it crept
    Nebulously, towards a sleepy strand,
Where nighted breezes, whispering, then swept
    The weird red fog into the dreamy land:

Unnatural, the fog was full of sighs;
    It soon engulfed the steeples, roofs and squares,
The cloud collecting souls with eerie cries
    Of smothered hope, dead dreams of dim despair

That settled in the folds of scarlet pall;
    And I beheld this like some mystagogue
    Who, couching on the moon, had seen the Earth

Immersed into a mist-borne burial,
    When, rising out the crimson gauze of fog
    Came laughter—though all mockful was its mirth.

Underlying Cause

John Shirley

Nature seeks out her victims
With a sad deliberation
Those she gifts with brilliant symptoms
Can't spurn the invitation

Artists, poets—writers like Joyce
Have no chance to decline the light;
no declining their destined voice—
Their wracking fits, the muscles tight

Why so many drunkard poets,
Why all the debauched painters?
Why so many antic writers,
Why so fragile—even fainters?

Yes some will vaunt a macho stance;
(Some will be women martyred)
But all are plagued by the horrid chance:
Seeing the world without blinders

When you peer without a blindfold,
You see before you all mankind:
They dance the mad tarantelle of olde;
—naturally you clutch at wine.

Red Thoughts

Simon MacCulloch

I will fall through the empty sky of her stare
To the pit that her shark teeth rim,
And I'll boil in the laughter bubbling there
Where the souls of her old loves swim
In the ebb and the surge of her whim.

My remains will hunt as a brittle husk
Through the halls of her castle-crypt,
Like a dog on the scent of the bitter musk
That the dream of her smile once dripped
On the heart that her red claws ripped.

Then I'll lay my skull on an altar-stone
Where a goat-faced priest presides,
And he'll stir the slime in the sphere of bone
Where the germ of my passion hides,
And I'll die, but the germ abides.

So soon you will watch as the stars are obscured
By the smoke as the hellfire catches,
And the oven heats red for the red thoughts lured
To this castle of heaven-made matches,
Till the egg of the lamia hatches.

Of Xenomorphs in the Black Abyss

Manuel Pérez-Campos

Whenever the dense zenith-dwelling towers which dominate
this square downtown mile are thrusted with spectacular
indifference into inscrutable passages
from the inhuman immensity of its nightside
cerulean there arise tenuously deep within the core
of my being as though wisps of convoluted
unreason all the hidden abominations
of transmundane worlds which lurk invisibly in it:
their half-heard screech spectrums make me feel
vertigo, for I am accosted then by an infinitude
of crumbling undefinable things that beg for release
from some principle of mercy that is not
forthcoming: and when the first light strengthens
within that night of spirits overpowered and it all
ceases, I sense it has not: and tremble.

A Rare Trait in Rabbits and Mice

Steven Withrow

Samantha Leveret's body—there's a fright!
You *have* been digging. Hutchins said you might
Not trust the doctor's full report. But to follow
The chain down here to *me*, it's hard to swallow.
Your paper can't be paying you that much,
Which means you're out of pocket here. Did Hutch
Point out that when they did the autopsy
I wasn't there? He skipped that part, did he?
(Can't say I blame him. *He* got the inside view,
And *I* came in to mop up all the goo . . .
Oh, Christ, there was so much of it.) My job?
A coroner's custodian—a slob
Who wipes the floors and tables in the morgue.
Sure, my degree's from Janitors-Dot-Org,
But I *listen* and I process what I hear
When forensics boys invite me for a beer
And start to let off steam about their cases.
You learn a lot by looking at their faces:
How badly mangled or how young the stiff,
If the car rolled over or barreled off a cliff.
(With corpses I don't like to get too close;
I think of them as being comatose
And needing rest, so I just let them sleep.

It got so I was scared to make a peep
When I was sweeping near their drawers alone.
I tiptoed, and I never brought my phone.)
"It almost wasn't human," one guy said
The night Samantha Leveret rolled in dead
To meet the scalpels and the surgical saws.
"But damned if I can't find another cause."
His buddy—that was Hutchins—also worked
Second shift. He sighed and sort of smirked:
"You're saying she was pregnant *with a litter,*
Like some giant rat or mutant bunny bit her,
Then her belly swelled past monster-movie girth
And trauma killed her before she could give birth?"
The first guy nodded. "It's called *superfetation.*
A divided womb, with serial gestation
Of embryos. As freakish as these are—"
A hockey game blared on above the bar,
And I could only watch their moving lips.
My stomach was already doing flips.
I wanted to shake them, beg them to explain,
But, even with the mess I'd cleaned, my brain
Kept sliding like a player on the ice.
(*"I've seen it once in laboratory mice . . ."*)
A rink's a kind of morgue; you keep it cold.
(*"This girl was barely seventeen years old . . ."*)

I stood and sprinted for the parking lot.
I drove home, quit my job. That's all I've got.
Use my quotes, but please don't use my name.
I'd like to be left out, if it's all the same.
These days? I'm working nights, driving a cab.
It's still with me. I pick at it like a scab.
It helps to talk, I guess. No, I don't pray.
If Heaven's there, then something's in our way.

Briar Rose

DJ Tyrer

Castle engulfed by vines and thorns
Twisting maze of ever-growing deceit
In which many a brave prince
Has been trapped to turn to bones
Until one makes it through the forest
By virtue of heart, steel, and flame
To reach the maiden's hidden tower
Where the Princess reclines in death-like sleep
Only to learn it is far too late
Princess is one now with her prison
Flesh transformed to spongy bark
No longer human but a true briar rose

After the Burning

Jacqueline West

Since she climbed down
from the pyre, unpeeled
shining skin from the post
and stretched shriveled
hands in their new black
gloves, dawn has slid to
night and back, the crows
and buzzards circled off
to look for quieter dead,
the scent of smoke thinned
fine as a veil. Already
flesh is thickening, coating
bones they could not burn
although they've tried
and tried again, and wild
white hair whips from
her head like seeds blown
on the ash-black wind.
She's done it before, sap
cracking scorched bark,
blood stirred to a boil,
what was old becoming
new. Some pines need

a forest fire. Watch the dew
hiss on her footprints.
Watch the green uncurl
from the singed ground.

Trapdoor Beneath the Feet of the Hanged Man

Kendall Evans

predawn sky
earth trembled
sudden explosion
guardian above

suddenly erupted
flee the wooden barrier
locking me inside
in terror, heat-choked

every breath
blistering
engulfed my sanctuary
mercifully

lost consciousness
dark-enveloped
boiling lava
ashen rock

this same loop
over and over

clawing my way
thru space and time

I'm still here
trapped forever
in an endless eternity
nighttime travelling

[Inspired by Ambrose Bierce's "An Occurrence at Owl Creek Ridge."]

Serpentine Stitch (Decaying Seams)

Eli Alemán

At first glance,
my needle fashions souls
into wearable, stylish attire—
its customizable surgical precision
will have you touching faith,
as if I were your personal confessional.

Self-anointed priestess of cloth and thread,
I do not care, but I do listen.
Each stitch a prayer for shorter lifespans—
still, I hold the secrets sacred.
My clients will never go to their graves
looking unkempt.

Alas, I hide the caveat:
every piece worn accelerates decay.
Word spreads; queues form.
They twirl in mirrors, grinning—
oblivious, as the silver serpent in my hand
feeds on their life force.

Arcane threads, forgotten rites,
my needle sings lullabies

in cadence with fading heartbeats.

Soulbind Stitch—imperceptible join,
tightens with motion,
siphoning vitality with every seam.
Egos drain, memories fatigue,
aliveness spills into hems.

My favorite to cut?
Joviality. It bleeds beautifully.
Heartstring weave,
embroidered to the beat,
a second skin over hollow bone.

Griefwear devours slowly:
bitterness is its sweetest nectar.
Every tear candies the fabric,
quickens the end.

Sleep offers no mercy—
dreamweave burrows into breath.
Necks cinch tight with ghostly thread.

Once they expire,
souls cling to filaments,

never snagging,
never free.

I ensure they remain
on all best-dressed lists.

Immortal Bird

David Barker

As in a dream, the weird bird called my soul
And led me to a black cone formed of stone
That rose above the frozen southern pole
Beneath whose icy gulfs the crystal shone.
A billion years ago, Yith's ancient priests
Sailed from their dying world past Neptune's moons,
Swapped minds with primal men and lesser beasts
They found half-starved in Earth's Antarctic dunes.

This realm was ruled by a nomadic race.
With time, fierce winds wore smooth its carven range.
Its towered city built by gods from space
Now mutely sleeps beneath deep snows most strange.
That mad bird squalled at me as if to warn:
"Don't stay too long—you'll wish you ne'er were born!"

[Inspired by H. P. Lovecraft's *Fungi from Yuggoth* sonnet "XV. Antarktos."]

The River Beneath the Floor

Flavia Pierret

Beneath the floor, there is a river.
It beats.
It moves like a heart without body.
I hear it when I go still,
and in its current drift shapeless things—
bits of her voice,
fragments of nails,
laughter that was once mine,
before it melted into the mastication of the soul.

Isn't that love?
To be one?
To be indivisible . . . even in digestion?

The Baleen Clock

Joshua Green

I place the artefact upon the dock,
And look above as stars then wink and die.
I wait for Her who hears the baleen clocks,
As ripples mirror death across the sky.

Beneath the water come Her subtle cries,
As tentacles erupt and break the lake.
Ascending faces open twelve wet eyes,
To stare upon the ticking clock and quake.

This woven keratin makes no mistake.
It ticks away and shows when She will fade.
We share a fear, and I approach to take
Her knowledge of my death and how it's made.

She stares upon the baleen clock. No breath.
Within Her eyes I see my coming death.

Dracacyn

Adam Bolivar

On a high cliffside   a hall roosted,
Its oak ancient: from elf-forests
The wood was felled,   the work of ettins,
Blood-drenched the beams.   Bold the youth was,
Who scaled skyward   to scry the hall
His dreams haunted.   Dracacyn bode there,
The earl of old,   though empty his court,
Cold and cheerless   as a cave's belly.
The folk cowered   in fear of their lord,
Boundless his craving   for the blood of men,
And warned Géac   to ware the hall
And stray not near.   Steadfast in purpose,
By the moon's brightness   he made his way
Over barren moorland   through a bleak passage
Threading briar   thickly growing,
Winding mazy.   Winsome in moonlight,
A girl waited   with a gift for Géac,
A rare dagger,   rowan-bladed,
To kill the fiend.   Courteous the earl was,
And Roman wine   of reddest tincture
In a goblet he poured   for the gallant strider
Who called that night.   In the cold guest-bed,
Dracacyn slithered   at dark midnight
To steal lifesblood   for strange hunger,
But the rowan blade   wreaked his downfall

When Géac stabbed him,   his yowls eerie,
Deft doombringer   the deathly strike,
And curse-breaking.   The canny maiden,
Dracacyn's daughter,   danced with the Gandring,
At a wedding wassail   on the wild heather,
The hall Géac's now,   and its heavy annals.

[Note: The name Géac—a speculative Old English version of Jack—is
pronounced *yawk*.]

Spirit Sleuth

A. J. Dalton

blink rapidly, stare
fixedly, relax your gaze
you'll see them

their shadows clustered
clinging to the ceiling
waiting for you to sleep

you'll struggle
to wake, dream-fuddled
exhausted and drained

you can't blame them
for not wanting to fade
out of existence entirely

yet they're not
your ghosts of lives
cruelly taken:

there must be a murderer
in the area dispossessing
bodies of their spirits

maybe a mumbling medium
can channel
something useful, for once

or better to do it yourself
door-to-door to explore
awkward absences and lonely silences

to discover clues or a pattern
as to what's happened
and what won't anymore

usually it's someone unblinking
but there are whispers of late
of a *something*

insatiable and inescapable
ancient and inexplicable
so I fear that I will find it

alone, alert or waiting
for me, as I'm tiring
and fully unexceptional

though there's a new priest in town
so young and fresh and sweet
succulent, some might say

an encumbrance probably
or an unholy coincidence
to arrive at such a time

but I'm out of friends and options
and maybe he's a sign:
God has sent me some help

at long bloody last.

The Ghosts That I See Are All My Own

Darrell Schweitzer

The ghosts that I see are all my own,
no celebrity specters, decapitated royalty,
or martyred presidents,
not even the befuddled Hessian soldiers
with which eastern Pennsylvania is allegedly replete.

My ghosts rise gently, as if from a dark pool.
I can almost make out their faces
before they sink down again and are gone,
like figures from a fading dream.

But I can hear them:
"Come," they say.
"Join us," they say.
"You are one of us," they say.

The ghosts that I see are all my own.

The Best Employee

Norbert Góra

Long hours shrink
to grains of sand,
the hourglass
has been turned
upside down again,
groans chase whispers,
bounce off the desks,
occupied forever
by ghosts, cadavers
and zombies
always in suites.
Dressed in the skin
of the committed challengers
for whom there will be
nothing left of the prize,
who gives money
to those blurred
in the memory
of the external world,
buried alive
in the urn of the absent,
who would like to
look at those empty eyes,
radiating the blue light
from the company laptop.

Excel tables are wider
than the universe,
reports are longer
than the sum of experiences,
results will take
the board to the financial heaven,
the attention will be focused on me,
the attention will be focused on me!
Still not enough, so little time,
the hourglass set in motion
repeatedly erases
the achievements
to start a new race
for the crown of the best employee.

a ubiquitous silence

Lee Clark Zumpe

I have beheld impossible hues
stacked in sedimentary layers
above ice-bound deserts
that stretch toward cold, distant horizons;

I have cowered beneath the void—
the intolerable blackness of night—
long after the last dwindling stars
deserted their designated constellations;

I have visited abandoned cities,
quickly crumbling into decay—
wandered amidst fallen monuments,
and slept among neglected graves;

I have heard the fading echoes—
the fury and clamor of civilization
reflected in stubborn, rusty machines
and slowly failing engines;

I have offered an elegiac tribute
to the grim inevitable,
the unraveling of all things,
and to the ubiquitous silence at the end.

Echoes in the Shade

Ngo Binh Anh Khoa

Time wilts away with each tick of the clock
Whose echoes stab the silent shroud of night—
Repeatedly as if to cruelly mock
The surging memories steeped in pain and fright
Of what's transpired within the strangling shade
That haunts this bed where I now lie, confined
Amid these walls and sheets, a helpless prey
Trapped in a serpents' pit. My racing mind
Grows madder with all senses heightened though
My limbs are like a corpse's, cold and numb;
The sheets stir, where pale fingers, slithering, go
Around my neck till breathless I become.
Wan spectral faces loom and smile at me
With blood-stained eyes that burn with vengeful glee.

This Dread Glimpse

David McLachlan

it is gone now
if it ever was

but as a child I was witness
to cosmic vistas
drowned in silhouettes
of a dying dream

but it was no dream

i can still feel
the cold cyclopean stone
on bare trembling feet

i can still hear
a throated echo dying
amongst silent vistas

i can still see
a bloated silver moon above
blood-red monoliths

those myriad-gemmed skulls
forgotten martyrs
with pitted cavernous eyes

seducing me
within their black-pocked night

what awesome grandeur
that nightmares hold

it is gone now
gone to us all
this dread glimpse lost
among measureless aeons

Autumn's Crown

Scott J. Couturier

Autumn comes to crown my brow—
With fiery leaves & rotten flowers,
Antlers of bucks & berries swollen—
Red twine of ivy from wild bowers.

Autumn comes to crown my brow—
As an awestruck supplicant I bow,
Receiving blessings of a thinning veil—
Reign ordained by ragged caw of crow.

Autumn comes to crown my brow—
Golden sunlight & nights of wonder,
Ancient powers abroad with might—
Halloween when all is torn asunder.

Autumn comes to crown my brow—
Woodsmoke & reek of rotting loam,
Croak of toad & spoken twilit spell—
Ghosts go flitting in evening's gloam.

Autumn comes to crown my brow—
Regent of seasonal sacral rites,
Throne a tombstone by asters strewn—
I revel with witch & undead wight.

*   *   *

Autumn comes to crown my brow—
Wreath of blooded briars & ruddy oak,
Dusk of a dying year my cloak—
Knell of midnight my waking chime.
With Queen Mab's Merry Folk I go,
& in ash groves swear a sealing vow—
Oaths older than sin, stone, & Time.

Apocalypse Kisses

Pixie Bruner

I. Freeze

The last human dream dies under tundra and permafrost
Subzero frozen currents of air
The Ice Age of all ice ages
The last we shall recount.
We cannot use our tongues—
Open mouths freeze, spittle icicles
Upon removing masks and ventilators,
We can never be warm again.
It starts with simple sluggishness
Drowsiness as the chill slips past bone into soul.
Blood thickens like water,
Just rest, lay your head down upon the stone pillow,
I will tuck you in with a blow. A gneiss kiss on your brow.

Refrigerator Mother Earth,
No solid water, the chipped ice nips back.
Our mufflered cheeks the only incarnadine,
Before the pallid,
Before the blue and black of necrosis.
Blood doesn't flow.
If gashed, no flow, there's bloom,
Just red slush blossoms from wounds.
The wind chills to fire.
Ice crystals hold our eyes open,

Ludovico Technique us as the world frosts over.
Ice floes predate, polar bearers of Doom,
Wildlife are Anthropocene memories,
Burned in their biology book entries
Just to provide warmth last Summer.
The tide is advancing glaciers,
Earth is the forgotten Vitamix making frozen daiquiris
Each human is becoming a Snowflake.
The promise of a Spring-future thaw.
The hard froze globes our eyes
Shall never see.

As we lie beneath a featherbed of freshly fallen snow,
Islands of flesh once supple,
Exiles from sun and cosmic radiation,
Cast off driftwood and detritus under siege.
The air reverberates with ice crystals,
How the last hours before exhaustion
Were spent bare, mad, desperate.
No blankets or insulation fort held back the frenzy,
As air seeped through seams and from dreams
From the narrow cracks and crevices—
The liminal spaces of a Final Cold War.
The tide could not be twisted nor turned,
We reminisced for ancient wood-burning stoves.

*   *   *

Darling! As a child, did your toes ever touch soft sand
As the icebergs stood sentinel upon the horizon
As you played along the shoreline of mortality?

Bundle with me now
Into the hard-packed powder,
The blizzard assures our handfasting by guide ropes.
We stumble into this shared grave,
Bootprints swept away with frost and frigidity,
Hidden heat shimmers in us though we
Became shadow puppets and ghosts long ago.

II. Fire

Scorched by the blazes humanity kindled,
Rebirth awaits under charcoal trails.
We are the firestarters,
We are failed thefts of lightning and flame.

We crisped the ghostly birches,
Their excoriated flesh peels
From their onlooking blackened eye bark,
Leaving just a copse of corpses.
Fire walled off arboreal memorial parks.
Come Spring, the mycelium network

Revives, the spores to fruiting bodies,
Gills ejaculate, nestle in, take root,
Sprout off of dead wood
Insectile automatons of conservation
Continue their new mission.
They gnaw, jaws lathe the skeletal branches
Still sparks the forest chorus—
Combust, crackle snap like cereal
Wild rooted spawn break,
Resurrectionists from wildfire crucibles.

On the last trail, Nature blazed,
We waltzed over the ashes of existence,
Giggles and tangled dancing drunkenly to
Who By Fire? It was always humanity.

Sweet one, how were you burned to ash?
Were words cinders on your lips before spoken,
As we flambéed to extinction?

Waltz on charcoal with me now,
Our feet soiled in cremains and syrup sweet
We waltz further to damnation.
Hidden saplings erupt from the sooted earth
Our bodies became lumber years ago.
We, mere specters, in a fresh wild wood.

A (Familiar) Cosmic Gathering

Maxwell I. Gold

Gather 'round the flames as songs uttered
'neath hushed voices and hooded faces
whose visages concealed more sinister plans
for some grand, twisted purpose.
They were nothing though,
no person or being of consequence
except for the fact they longed to sing
to the lost gods to see them smile so widely
that it might rip the heaven's asunder;
and spoke gleefully of dead gods,
buried temples and ancient curses
scattered to the hideous stars whereupon the broken
remnants lay at their feet.
Trapped in the shadow-nethers in places
where death and dank dreams
forever dance in infinite duets,
they continued to sing
'round the pitiful flame in some nameless wood
and still, the fire burned as the stars grew ever distant.

The woods swayed in pallid twilight sky,
cautious arbiters trembling as if something
were to fell them by the very roots.
And yet, through the dirt covered mouths,
the hooded ones continued to sing

to the dark hearts and black stars,
beckoning that which was stirred awake
below the humble flame.
A dreadful beast so bleak and baleful,
spawned by the Cyber Gods,
upon the final note sung and sorrowful dawn,
nothing remained except the wistful ashes
from a familiar, cosmic gathering
'round some pathetic campfire in a nameless wood.

Homecoming

Silvatiicus Riddle

Autumn is a friend that I haven't seen in so very long.
It bounds over the land to greet me where I lay,
and I bury my face in its forest of cool fur.
It brings to me the smells of a darkening world,
of soil and loam, damp earth beneath tired feet,
of mist and hearth-fire and cinnamon bark.
Its breath is warm, and I know it's just eaten the sun.
I never wish to let it slip away again, and gather it close,
a beast so great I cannot tightly hold—soft as wind,
and grey as the long nights that stretch on ahead.
I find its gaze. There are ravens in my eyes.
My voice trims the air like smoke,
only a whisper to say:
"Welcome home."

Blinding

Nicholas De Marino

Skinned alive, we shadowkin stare down
nine millimeters of dawn. Clarity is nigh.

Flee. Occult your star-pocked flesh in cracks,
scrape across corners, dive underfoot.

Too late. Straddle reality. Delineate. Endure
prismatic violence and draconian geometry.

Focus on the rumbling throttle—the nihility
between clock ticks and insect clicks.

Freeze your faith as lucidity howls. Soon
obsidian will restore silent void.

Can you not hear? Space whispering
aswim in liquid possibility.

Brave cruel, ghoulish light. Fear not. For
day promises night. Icy, inky peace is coming.

Extinction

Michael Potts

Beneath the waters of the Southern Sea
the sandy bottom shifts and starts to rise—
Cthulhu floods the scene with dream-filled eyes
as twisted tesseracts break through a seal.
Deniers tell themselves, too blind to see,
Cthulhu is a myth—it's only lies.
Cthulhu laughs, his arms a twisted vise,
escaped from R'lyeh's ocean prison free.
Human beings asleep, oblivious
to Fate consigned, extinct in all but name—
brains sucked apart by tooth-filled tentacles,
re-formed, forced into empty vesicles—
no trace remains of human animals.

Tribe

Allan Rozinski

Here we stand on hallowed ground,
where the blood of our ancestors
has steeped down deep into the soil
like a torrent of unending tears.

In a world gone mad, we were the
last tribe seeking the way of peace;
we extended our hand in friendship
to other tribes, freely offering our aid.

But they regarded our stance as weakness,
and instead, as though possessed,
reveled in war, attacking every other
tribe in what seemed their monstrous quest

to plunder and seize all that came
into view with murderous rapture,
dreaming further of the unseen lands that lay
beyond new horizons made for capture.

With their blind and boundless lust
for blood and conquest,
we must now consider other means
to save what remains of the last of our kind.

In the distant past, our tribe once ruled the earth
with a ruthless hand, but at great cost;
we came to a fork in the road of our plight
and vowed to turn away from our sorcery.

But over time, our tribe became weak and small,
while our enemies draw closer with grim resolve;
they have stalked and now further surround us,
threatening to deliver us unto oblivion.

In this desperate hour, despite our vow to refrain
from summoning dark forces to subvert their ways,
we now have no choice but to again
call upon the Ancient Ones for aid.

So, we pray to you now, O Dark Gods.
Avenge us! Descend upon our enemies
like a storm of savage, ravenous wolves,
like a whirlwind of festering plague;

destroy and mete out suffering upon
those whose eyes see nothing
but the objects of desire that reflect their greed,
whose ears will listen to nothing

but their own confounding noise and lies;
let order again be restored to the world,
and give power once more to us,
your loyal warriors of the Original Tribe.

Invasion from the Worst of All Possible Worlds

Manuel Pérez-Campos

Having swelled beyond all reckoning just outside
the most inaccessible part of our dreams, which
is where the abomination which it has always
been exists, it has broken through at last unbeknownst
to us and begun to translocate our affairs
into the invisible whorls of its intensive
end-of-days events. It is as an untimely
downpour-spewing darkness that it has come
without tact at me, a hunched misanthrope
who feels as though he were being hallucinated
holding on to hat and overcoat by the screech
of leaves along the teetering elms of a boulevard.
I exult in the dissentient power being
deposited in my brain by the voluminous
all-penetrable howl of eons which never were
turning the cumbrous laberynth of sidewalks
into an absence most exhilarating: colossal
sections ahead of me that were awaiting
my arrival are being dismantled and their once
luminous debris dispersed until I forget
language and all I see dissipates into a schemeless
scheme: and then a slim rectangular hole
opens in my forehead as I sense neutralized

that it has turned me into a dim unalive
gate and that through it are fluxing forth
with spontaneous impetuous might inimical to the modes
of expression of humanity the tenebrific ill-
boding inwardnesses of inhuman
incorporealities, each of whose inalienable
wickedness dwarfs the entire planet's.

Theobald Vesselldoom: An Albino Four-Leaf Clover

Wade German

I. Moth Tower

I thought the lonely, mouldered place
    Abandoned even by its ghosts;
Thus so, methought to haunt its space—
    To welcome by a million hosts.

And every night they proselytize
    Their olden worship of the moon;
Now I, become most insect-wise,
    Behold each midnight for my noon.

But all around the tower rots,
    Its ancient bones beset with damp—
Moistening all the mothy thoughts
    Which flicker round my moony lamp.

II. Charon's Obols

Old Charon steered his haunted barge
    With many a gloomy ghost on board;
I, too, had paid the ferrying charge,
    But wondered: where might lie his hoard?

Surely, he hid his untold wealth.
    If locked in some vast vault of Hell,
Was it accessible by stealth,
    Protected by Plutonian spell?

Those obols, each by corpse tongue kissed,
    In silvery mountains surely rise;
Perhaps a few might not be missed
    To spend beneath Hell's earthen skies . . .

Charon still steered our floating hearse,
    Slowly, but surely hellward on—
Then paused mid-stream, there took his purse
    And tossed it in the Acheron.

III. Exaltation of Moss

Thou life form, living since primeval time
    On Earth—and elsewhere surely taken hold,
As thou survivest in most every clime—
    So simple is thy wisdom very old:
Through slow and subtlest action, take thy need
    In toothless feast upon the marble stone
Of holy houses, and the tombs to feed
    Thy sleepless rest upon the sighing bones;
And moistured by the sylvan misted dew,
    Breed space where mindless creatures creep and crawl,
Soft turf of amethyst or emerald hue—
    Thou lowly, blithe colossus, conquer all
        In velvet blankets that consume the dead,
        And gnaw away the world beneath thy spread.

IV. Dead Magic

Thy mystery has been revealed,
    The secrets whispered, then retold;
The holy wisdom thine to wield
    A dwindled sun now, dim and cold.

Thy deities are dead as dreams
    Dissolved in waking nothingness;
Their holy hymnals to us seem
    Mere séance-summoned emptiness.

Thy sacred flame, the great ideal,
    The wonder, and thy mystic thought—
Unreal, once reified, is real
And subject to the ways of rot:

Thou mummy from an old-world tomb,
    A monarch or magician proud,
Now phantom of museum rooms
    Profaned by pleasure-seeking crowds.

Her Ways

Jay Hardy

Molly's body
Hangs nearby.
It has
Neither eye.
Both plucked
Long ago
By some
Hungry crow.
She sees
Despite that
Through her
Black cat.
Molly dangles
Midair.
It wanders
Everywhere.
It returns
Faithfully
Whispering under
Her tree.

Molly listens
And learns
As she
Slowly turns.

She plans.
We wait
Recalling well
Her hate.
Witches never
Truly die.
Only she
Knows why.
Molly's cat
Repeats well
The gossip
Folks tell.
We avoid
Their gaze
Familiar with
Her ways.

Honorary God

Jay Sturner

The moon has come up over the mountains like a blind eye. The townsfolk in the valley are locking their doors and closing their curtains.

The heartbeat of the earth gallops like a hunted unicorn.

In one of the cottages, a young woman paints runes across her naked breasts. In another, a young man paints similar runes across his muscular arms. Each puts a small rune atop their eyelids. The final touch is a rune over each temple.

When ready, the man and woman peer out of their windows to the empty road.

A shape quietly enters the village; the shape is that of a robed figure with a book in one hand and a heavy cross in the other.

Man and woman appear on the road; they block the way of the shape. Moonlight breaks through the pines like fairy shine, knits the man and woman together. Out of a swelling mist, two become one: an honorary god.

Without a word the god grabs and swallows the robed figure.

The heartbeat of the earth slows to a quiet calm.

Uphill from the village, the figure is coughed out, told never to return.

Less and less now do the self-righteous dare enter such places—those regions in which the ancient ways have made their return.

Baba Yaga

Christian Dickinson

A treble screeching tears across the sky
As twilight falls upon the silent wood.
The pilgrim seeks some shelter, safe and good
To flee from shining eyes in darkness nigh.

The strangest sight appears before his view:
A hut upon a pair of feathered legs—
Enclosed not by a fence of wooden pegs,
But bones and skulls, with sheerest pale-white hue

The pilgrim enters, eager for respite,
And sees a shadow rise before the fire.
A face looks up: a wrinkled, hooded crone's
And in the cauldron's broth, the smallest bones.
"Come in my dear and sate your sharp desire!"
The pilgrim runs, as cackles fill the night.

The Diver

Alper Ghuchlu

Scuba diver sees
A coral reef
So beautiful
He decides to touch
Eyes open
A giant creature is unleashed
The diver frozen
"Worry not, curious human,
 you're the one to set me free."
 Its voice a terrible rasp
 Ringing in his ear
"For this, you will be my messenger.
 Find all who will worship me,
 they too shall be spared.
 I give you five weeks.
 Until that time, farewell."
 It retreats into the ocean
 Once again a coral reef
 Diver unsure what to do
 At least he could try
 Hopelessly

After Perrault

Geoffrey Reiter

The beast broods by the tangled path to pause
With slav'ring fangs until he sees a red
Bright slash of wool, the drool aglint on jaws
That hum with hunger. Padded paws then tread
The wood till he can steal into the bed
When that fresh girlish flesh steps through the door.
Another beast who haunts another bed
Has locked another door. Where one wolf wore
An older woman's weeds, this beast is more
Sophisticate in fashion—breeches, coat
And cuffs, enough to squelch the stench of gore
That crusts on rusty hinges, where the throat
Of each dead wife lies rent. So tell me, then,
Which is the fiercer beast among the men?

Breakout

Simon MacCulloch

I swore to the bitch I'd be back;
No poison sufficient to kill me
When vengefulness floods in to fill me.
My eyes are blind now, but I *will* see
Though coffin and grave paint them black.

My coffin-cramped limbs scrape and claw
This satin-soft quilt that enfolds me,
This dark fetid prison that holds me
And slowly, remorselessly moulds me
To something I wasn't before.

Before, when I trusted my wife
To love, honour, and obey me;
Refused to believe she'd betray me,
Sequester my wealth and repay me
By putting an end to my life.
An end, though she carried my son!
But demon-bought magic will save me;
Though powers of darkness enslave me,
I'll have the revenge that I crave, free
To finish what she has begun.

It's finished; I burst from my cell
And see, coiling redly around me,
The raw bloody bonds that had bound me.

My demon delights to confound me
With unforeseen versions of hell—

A hell for that bitch as I ripped
Through walls that I thought had entombed me:
The flesh of my wife that enwombed me.
Revenge through rebirth, but it's doomed me
To strangle, my life-cord unsnipped.

Encounter

DJ Tyrer

It brushes along the hull
Caressing the submarine
Making love to the steel beast
Arms snaking about it
With an awesome strength
Rivet-popping power
Fountains of spray
Structural integrity fails
The submarine implodes
Crumpling like tin foil
Exposing the flailing crew
To probing tentacles
That snatch and seize
Depositing the fleshy contents
Into a vast, insatiable maw
Then releases its grip
Lets the mangled wreckage drift
Down into the mud
Of the abyssal plain

Dormant Knoll

Steven Withrow

Sheep avoid it still, that small round hill
The Puritans and Wampanoags let sleep,
As if the dormant knoll possessed a will
To counter the advance of browsing sheep.

Four hundred winters later, boys with sleds
Ignored their elders' warnings, climbed the mound
(What foolishness creeps into children's heads!)
And were, despite our searching, never found.

The knoll is as it was, when Pilgrim wives
Or Sachem's daughters picked no nettles there,
And passing birds are quick to guard their lives;
A wedge of geese keeps safely to the air.

And a hiker from the city swears he heard
The peal of boyish laughter from the knoll:
"So shrill, it might have been a hunting bird,
But it was *human*. Christ, it chilled my soul."

Dies Irae

Andrew Paul Wood

An asylum where no patient now remains,
Its atrium lies gaping to the void,
Where, pasteboard-masked, a man recites the names
To mannequins, of gods now long-destroyed.
He points aloft and claims the sky a wound
That never heals; his feigned despair is fake;
His cities dreamed to death, submerged, entombed;
The soul, he claims, a clerical mistake,
Made in a mindless demiurge's rage.
He offers neither counsel nor laments.
This is his final haven—and his cage.
Outside, the wind bears sharp and souring scents
Of trite nostalgia, rot, and formalin.
Inside, the dust pretends it's listening.

In Darkness

Adam Bolivar

In darkness shone a phantom light,
    An eidolon beyond,
A distant dancer, stark and white,
    Who held me in a bond.

I heard it calling out to me,
    The voice each night I dreamed,
And closer still I stole to see
    This dancing light which gleamed.

Was it the lantern held by Jack,
    An omen of my doom,
A shepherd gravely robed in black,
    To guide me to my tomb?

A woman, rather, beckoned me,
    In whitest silk arrayed;
Beneath a veil I could not see
    The features of this maid.

And so I lifted up her veil
    To view my ghostly bride,
Then kissing lips as opals pale,
    My final breath I sighed.

The Face in the Night-Shrouded Window

John Shirley

The face in the window
cruelly cognized
The dark glassy face
Black-ink incised

It is my own face;
Then again it is not—
It's more like a mood,
just trapped and caught;

A crushed skullish moth
'neath microscope clamps
A face cut from strange cloth
seen under dim lamps:

It's the ghost of the future
(say voices, behind)
A translucent vulture;
Yet a man of a kind

Its eyes are but shadow
mouth etched in a frown
A terribly gaunt face
Its features drawn down

It seems but a portent
(come muttering voices)
a kind of a portrait—
of unmindful choices . . .

To a Distant Star

Jason Ray Carney

Upon the firmament, that map of night,
Where silent stars in chilly aether gleam,
I trace a solace in their pallid light,
And lose the world within a waking dream.

The Ancients saw their heroes, snatched away,
To burn as legends, ne'er to feel the sun;
A stolen boy, for whom the gods would pray,
Whose grace a cold and deathless glory won.

So seems thy sphere, a truth serene and vast,
A mind that scorns the passions of the day,
A steady pole when frantic storms are cast,
A quiet port from this world's disarray.

Let others seek the sun's intemperate fire,
My soul finds peace in what they deem so dire.

Of Feathers and Vows

Eli Alemán

Clip the veil secure and firm,
clasp the lace barrettes shut,
perfectly coiffed jet hair,
each feathered wisp meticulously placed—
the ultimate test:
will you make the bride cry?

Liquid salt diamonds spill down her décolletage,
joyous gullet swelling under her skin.
Bride, veil, and dress—
a trinity of matchmaking approval.

Behind her, the entourage stands stiff.
Bridal mantilla thick with crow feathers,
silk buried under oily indigo sheen—
something borrowed, something blue.

Box-wrapped Chantilly gift,
carried onto her from nowhere.
They whisper: a siege of misfortunes,
each barb a rachis of occultism.
But the bride with black-blushed cheeks
sees vintage beauty.
The groom smiles his assent.

A fortnight to the wedding.

Hair clumps ring her feet—
no bald spots, only a molt.
Lips peel; blood touches tongue.
Shoes discarded.
Thickened skin tears at the corners of her mouth.

She slathers on Grandma's remedies,
the ones that earned the snug diamond ring.
Her eyelids shrink in silk-lined sleep—
not enough skin left to shut her eyes.

A week away.
Her back a field of trenches,
eyes too wide,
seeing forbidden colors.
The groom enters, smiling,
touches her plumage as if it were satin.
He kisses the crude black beak.
She prays for death.

"Sing for me," he whispers.
Only caws emerge.
Still, he smiles.

The night before:
she perches on taloned feet,

retches from peppermint perfume.
The white dress hangs—
its glow insults her.
It is not kin to the veil.
It is enemy.

At the altar, guests scatter.
She hops the aisle, chirping warnings.
Veil and dress at war.
White stained, dulled.

The groom lifts the veil.
An avian face weeps beneath.
Still, he says, "I do."

Later, she plucks a single feather
to stitch into the veil
after consummation.

Dr. Frankenstein's Electro-Mechanical Monster

Kendall Evans

Dr. Frankenstein's
Latest model
An electro-mechanical Monster
Of the female persuasion

Created and stitched together
To appease the male monster
Who had been killing
Kindly innocent blind folk

And children
And ravishing the Arctic Wilderness—
However
When she lured him inside

Her
It was shocking
Electrifying
They ejected

Electro-plasma Energies
Together
And the truth of it is
Afterwards

The male Frankenstein's
Or is it Frankenstein's
Male monster
Never felt

Like a monster
No, not ever
Never
Again

the wily moon

Lee Clark Zumpe

should the wily moon stray
from its heavenly course,
casting uncanny shadows

across the forested valley
beneath two towering summits
of that grim and stately mountain;

should that uncanny glow
infiltrate the wooded realm
strewn with megalithic tombs and cairns—

immense, mysterious monuments,
dating back before recorded history,
when forgotten tribes dwelled here;
should the cunning stars swing
far afield, vacating their residency
to reconfigure the firmament

in such choreographed anarchy
that perturbations ripple
through the dreams of sensitive bohemians;

should night be subverted,
if only temporarily,
what barriers will be breached?

                    *   *   *

what terrible raptures will be shared,
what aguish and what ecstasies arise?
what misshapen gods will seek veneration?

A Dread Cycle Renewed

David McLachlan

Out they came,
whispers of a death promise,
flaming phosphorescent crowns,
unhallowed eyes shining
with profane lust
and glimpses of unspeakable cruelty,
bare muscled chests still painted
with the bright crimson spray
of arterial blood.
Their jagged obsidian blades
flashed in the malignant light.
The red moon quivered
with forgotten satiety
when the corybantic screams
began anew,
when the severed beating hearts
were raised once more
to a welcoming god.

Fu-Pao, the Witch of the Northern Lights

Arukoya Tomais

Fu-Pao, of the Yougiao Clan
Was left much alone as a child
Unsupervised, fell into bad company
At the age of eight
Initiated as a witch—

But the witch of what
Or whichever? For she had no powers,
At that early age, to define her—
Often scoffed at, by the other witches—
Until, of a single fateful night

She chanced to observe
The northern lights,
A transformative incident
For she, beguiled,
Immediately fell in love

This inexplicably beauteous phenomena!
—And it should be mentioned
Contrary to common expectations
Few witches truly possess
The rarified power of flight

* * *

But Fu-Pao, immersed
In the aurora of the northern sky,
Drifted aloft effortlessly
Riding her mighty yet imaginary mount
A creature formed
From the wavery, waving curtains
Of supernal radiance—
She named him Yáoyuǎn de Hēiàn,
Far Darkness,
Because the spectral stallion

Was the opposite exact,
A spirited stallion
Fashioned out of light and radiance—
And she gracefully rode him
Night after night after night

Yet she could only ride the waves,
The tides of light,
In the presence of
The Aurora Borealis
When Yáoyuǎn de Hēiàn appeared

And she leapt to his bare back
And plied the eight skies above,

Alone with the elements; rapturous—
Er long the belly of the virgin witch
Began to swell with pregnancy

Appropriate, since she has already
Professed her love
Of and for the spirits
Of the Northern Aurora
And all its sky-dancing elementals.

She passed the next
Ten months joyously
Before giving birth to a celestial child
Destined to become
The Emperor of China, Huang Di,

Known as the Yellow Emperor
Who singlehandedly
Rallied the Han Chinese
To oppose and overthrow
The oppressive Quin Dynasty—

How her life has changed,
Fu Pao, now honored
As Huang Di's mother
Her life in the court

Cushioned, protected, obeyed—

And yet, by night,
When she rides the eight skies above
She is the same witch as she ever was
Riding the waves of the Northern Lights
Mounted upon fierce Yáoyuǎn de Hēiàn

Picture her there in the sky
Surrounded by fiercely charged particles
Aglow, alive, triumphant
Her long wavy hair standing upright on end
Much like that of a monster's bride.

k.t.u.l.k.h.u

Yuliia Vereta

a myth fossilized before myths were born.
it surfaced in no scripture, yet every ruined temple
left space for its shadow.

not a god—but a question the universe once asked itself,
then buried under aeons of unknowing.

its bones are not found in earth
but in instinct—
the shape of dread in children's dreams,
the silence between radio pulses,
the echo beneath time's first scream.

Wicked Imp

Janice Klain

you wicked little imp
torturing us while shuffling along
far from oblivious
far from human

you wicked little imp
claiming knowledge
far from communicative
far from human

you wicked little imp
doing nothing but glaring
far from this world
far from human

you wicked little imp
your boundless frothing evil has no place here
so far from good
so much farther from human

Surf's Up

Nicholas De Marino

Death comes for me
in a swimsuit cover-up.

"Dude," I plead.
DUDE, it replies.

An ocean of sand but
the hourglass is sealed—

no cheating or ghosting
this bone dry specter.

I plant my board upright
as a tombstone as

Death wraps its scythe blade
in beach bag canvas.

Wallet's in the glove box;
no coinage, no ferryman.

We wade into the surf,
rolling rolling rolling.

Widowspins

Oliver Smith

A dryad with acorns in her maddened hair
scrubbed out the sorrow from a deadman's shirt;
left it dangling from the birches' green twigs.
His wraith basked beneath the pale cotton flag;
brimstone-winged in the summer glade.

Once, hunting he came; all bones and rags.
She might have been his maytime-queen
filled with the surly innocence of summer's youth.
He might be the wild bee in orbit;
a moth upon her midnight bloom.

Her heart grows softer in the dog-days
whose cumulous heads burst in evening thunder.
The Babel-streams gush between livid banks
and the remains of her lost lover are crowded
with a feast of flies in metal-blue.

A sad old sun descends in a blood-swamped sky
of new rekindled fire. She asks the year to turn
until pale-morning wakes her; turn until
ruffian winter calls the woods to sleep,
turn until it can turn no more.

On Golden Gate Bridge

Manuel Pérez-Campos

It darts through waves beside inverted
seagulls like a thing of shining perseverance
which threatens to depart to the horizon
and whose only purpose is to connect prospects
of limitlessness with passing voices: but when
an ill-omened night arrives and its daunting arches
disappear, it is felt as something different:
as an envoy of sea demons, a dangerous
corridor of briny scent that has solidified
out of an ascended fog at the edge of a
neverness and that during the slightest
changes of wind whistles to whoso demand
guidance from its wavering far-off lights without
proper obeisance to that powerful lord of the
insidiously unknowable whose outer manifestation
it is of darkling destinations to come.

Bury Her

Scott J. Couturier

She died by her own hand—
No interment on church land
For her. A plain pauper's plot,
By an old, gnarled willow—
Well know I the spot!
There I've buried unbaptized babes,
& those of blasphemer's lot.

She died by her own hand—
It was poison: it was planned.
Thwarted in her love's attainment,
She downed strychnine &
Donned black raiment—
See! Even now she smiles,
Death's over-joyous claimant!

She died by her own will—
Dig her grave deep, & fill
It up with weighty stones & chaff.
Should she waken to
Unholy life she'll laugh
& count out each pesky grain
Before rising on bloodlust's behalf.

Classic Reprints

The Ghost

Mary Sharon

There is a ghost that walks for me,
    A Presence that I dread;
The Spirit of the Youth I was,
    Before my dreams were dead.

I sit before my study fire,
    While shadows writhe along the wall,
And Spirit hands rap on the door,
    And ghostly feet glide down the hall.

Outside my window, lifeless trees
    Lift fleshless fingers to the sky,
The night wind whistles eerily,
    Its moaning echoes will not die.

This ghost of mine will not be laid,
    Time cannot set me free;
It is the wraith of dear dead days,
    That comes to torture me.

[First published in *Weird Tales* (February 1924).]

The Parrot

Alfred Noyes

When the king and his folk lay dead,
    And the murderous hordes had gone,
He gnawed through his cage and fled
    To the swallowing woods alone;
But, after an endless age,
    He was taken by man once more;
And swung in a sturdier cage
    By a sun-bleached wine-house door.

And there, on a hot white noon,
    From his place on the blistered wall,
He whistled a dark old tune
    And called, as a ghost might call,
Farlo–Merillo–Rozace,
    With a chuckle of impish glee,
The words of the vanished race
    That none knew now but he.

Farlo–Merillo–Geray!
    And the spell-struck listeners heard
The tongue of the dead that day
    Talking again in a bird;
And his eyes were like blood-red stones,
    For round him the wise men drew,
And coaxed him with terrapin bones
    To tell them the words he knew.

Sleek as a peach was his breast,
      His long wings green as palms;
And, whiles, like a prince he'd jest,
      Then, beggar-like, whine for alms;
And, whiles, like a girl in flight
      He'd titter, then mimic a kiss,
And chuckle again with delight
      In that wicked old way of his.

He'd courtesy low, and he'd dance
      On his perch, and mockingly leer,
And stiffen himself and prance
      For the grey-beards listening there;
And once—O, dreadful and wild,
      In the blaze of that noonday sun,
He shrieked, like a frightened child
      That into the dark had gone.

[Taken from Noyes's *Dick Turpin's Ride and Other Poems* (New York: Frederick A. Stokes Co., 1927).]

Articles

Clark Ashton Smith: Before *The Star-Treader*

S. T. Joshi

Clark Ashton Smith created a sensation when, at the age of nineteen, he published *The Star-Treader and Other Poems* (1912), whose brilliance inclined reviewers to compare him with Keats, Shelley, Chatterton, and other poetic prodigies. But Smith had been writing verse for years before the appearance of this first volume. Throughout his teenage years he wrote large quantities of verse, much of it set in Arabia or India and inspired by Edward FitzGerald's translation of the *Rubaiyat* of Omar Khayyam, the poetry of Rudyard Kipling, and other sources.

But it was the poetry Smith wrote during 1910–11, much of which remained unpublished in his lifetime, that displayed the remarkable poetic development he underwent at this time.

Smith declares that he read George Sterling's "A Wine of Wizardry" ("in the pages of the old *Cosmopolitan*"[1]) two years after he discovered Poe (i.e., 1908), but he actually read the poem soon after its magazine appearance, since it had attracted so much attention throughout the state (and, to some degree, in the rest of the country) almost immediately upon its publication. But even if this is the case, it is incredible that this poem—and others by Sterling that Smith claims he hunted out in all the periodicals he could find—exercised not the slightest influence upon his juvenile verse. That influence only manifested itself in the poems Smith

---

1. "George Sterling—An Appreciation" (*Overland Monthly*, March 1927).

began to write in 1910. And yet, in later years he continued to speak of the poem's effect upon his own work:

> "A Wine of Wizardry" had great influence on my own poetic development, and helped my flair for the fantastic. I think it is the longest poem that I know entirely by heart. I first read it when it appeared in the "Cosmopolitan," about 1907, with an accompanying eulogy by Ambrose Bierce, who ranked it among the greatest imaginative poems in literature. To this I subscribe whole-heartedly, in the teeth of all the proper and grand Moguls of poetic (?) realism.[2]

It was at this time that Smith cast aside almost entirely his fascination with Arabia, India, and Persia and focused (perhaps without consciously realising it) on the "pure poetry" that Sterling and Ambrose Bierce had championed. The work that he wrote in 1910–11, before and during the first phase of his involvement with Sterling, presents such a radical break with his earlier work that it comes as a bracing shock—and it was this work that inaugurated the most remarkable phase of his poetic career, extending over the next decade and a half.

It was now that Smith looked back to the Romantic poets, Poe, and Sterling as his natural forebears and models. In acknowledging his debts to the Romantic poets he primarily had Keats and Shelley in mind. As he wrote to Sterling in 1912, "Keats and Shelley are in the first rank of greatness, and I'm only in the second rank, at best."[3] It was Shelley in particular whose challenge of religious orthodoxy and evocation of something approaching the cosmic—especially in the poetic drama *Prometheus Unbound* (1820)—evoked deep sympathy in Smith. He almost never mentions or cites the work of Lord Byron or William Wordsworth, and even the early Coleridge of "Kubla Khan" (1797) and *The Rime of the Ancient Mariner* (1798) does not seem to have touched his

---

2. CAS to Donald Wandrei, 6 December 1926; in *To Worlds Unknown: The Letters of Clark Ashton Smith, Donald Wandrei, Howard Wandrei, and R. H. Barlow*, ed. David E. Schultz and S. T. Joshi (New York: Hippocampus Press, 2023), 44–45.

3. CAS to George Sterling, 8 August 1912; in *The Shadow of the Unattained: The Letters of George Sterling and Clark Ashton Smith*, ed. David E. Schultz and S. T. Joshi (New York: Hippocampus Press, 2005), 55.

psyche significantly. William Blake's fusion of poetry and pictorial art would seem to make him a significant predecessor of Smith; and while Smith speaks warmly of Blake on a number of occasions, I see little influence of this singular English poet upon his work.

The influence of Poe—a master of horror poetry as well as horror fiction—might seem obvious, but it should be borne in mind that Smith's own poetry, with a number of exceptions, cannot be termed horrific in the strictest sense. His devotion to "cosmic" poetry is not at all derived from Poe, although no doubt Poe's poetry as a whole was a keen imaginative stimulus to Smith. He would also find inspiration in such of Poe's contemporaries as Thomas Lovell Beddoes (*Death's Jest-Book*, 1850) and John Clare, a poet of the English rural countryside who was in the process of being rediscovered during the early twentieth century. Smith also relished the poetry of James Thomson ("B. V."), whose *The City of Dreadful Night* (1880) was just about the last word in philosophical pessimism. Wilde's "The Sphinx" long remained a favorite poem of Smith's. He also probably read Swinburne extensively. In 1913 he began an ode to Swinburne, but never completed it, and the fragment does not survive. Nevertheless, he unhesitatingly declared that "Swinburne is the greatest of the Victorians."[4]

Whatever the case, the poetry of 1910–11 is a remarkable body of work. Only a few of these poems ended up in his first published book, but they are all pieces that emphasized the power of the human imagination (sometimes from a cosmic perspective) and the beauties of nature as a symbol for the beauty that life itself offers; some even dwell on horror and the supernatural.

"Imagination," a 108-line poem written in a somewhat unusual metre—stanzas of nine lines in an *ababbcbcc* rhyme scheme—is emblematic of Smith's paean to the imagination. Later in the poem a cosmic element definitely appears:

> Of other worlds thy wings ambitious are:
> O'er airless gulfs that yawn past reach of Day—

---

4. CAS to Samuel Loveman, 22 August 1913; in *Born under Saturn: The Letters of Samuel Loveman and Clark Ashton Smith*, ed. S. T. Joshi and David E. Schultz (New York: Hippocampus Press, 2021), 17.

Unfathomed voids of space 'twixt star and star,
    Unhesitantly thou dost essay
Some world exclusive from the sun's wide sway.
    Strange forms of life thine eyes thereon descry—
New, unfamiliar,—that yet tread a way,
    Which, dim and difficult, like ours doth he
Through dark and pain, toward goals that gleam in unity.[5]

"Ode to Matter," written in 1911 and consisting of 56 lines, may be the first harbinger of the cosmic odes that would bring him celebrity in 1911-12. Smith appeared to refer to it when he wrote to Sterling: "I've been trying my hand at some cosmic verse lately. . . . This is about what I've done in four poems, varying in length from 112 to 45 lines."[6] Smith also wrote a 46-line "Ode on Matter"; it is unclear which poem was written first.

"The Suns and the Void" is also cosmic, but much less impressive than "Ode to Matter." However, "The Fanes of Dawn" is an exquisite sonnet portraying the dawn, with hints of cosmicism ("where the cloudy fanes aspire / That house the visioned morning's purple flare, / And with it melt upon the crystal vast"), where "vast" is used distinctively as a noun. In "The Castle of Dreams," the realm of the imagination is depicted as the place where the "cares of Life are all forgot." Cosmicism also enters into "A Dream of Oblivion" and "Sonnet on Oblivion." Whether we are to see the influence of Sterling in these poems—given that one of the older poet's most celebrated works was "Three Sonnets on Oblivion," in A *Wine of Wizardry and Other Poems*—is unclear. The overall theme that oblivion overtakes all the vaunted monuments of the human race is common to both poems, but Sterling's is far more firmly grounded in human history ("Sargon is dust, Semiramis a clod!" is the opening line of the second sonnet, "The Dust Dethroned"), while Smith's poems underscore the cosmic: the final line of the sonnet speaks memorably of "A vast Nirvana of the universe."

---

5. All poems quoted here are found in Smith's *Complete Poetry and Translations*, ed. S. T. Joshi and David E. Schultz (New York: Hippocampus Press, 2007-08; 3 vols.).

6. CAS to George Sterling, 21 May 1911; *Shadow of the Unattained* 25.

"The Tartarus of the Suns" links cosmicism with references to classical myth, as the Titans, Zeus, and Pan are cited. It should be observed that Smith's poems of this early period generally lack such references, which were a commonplace in the Romantic poets—notably Shelley, Keats, and Swinburne—whom he presumably took for his models. At a later date the Titans do make significant appearances in Smith's verse, along with Nereids, the river Lethe (as a symbol of both forgetfulness and oblivion), and a few others.

Smith's nature poems are some of his most poignant. "To a Yellow Pine," "A Sierran Sunrise," "The Sierras," and "To a Mariposa Lily" all evoke the natural landscape of his native region. The mariposa lily is a genus of lily that is found all along the western edge of the American continent, extending from British Columbia to Guatemala; at least twenty-eight species are found in California alone. The flower is generally white or yellow, which is why Smith refers to it as "Wrought of the finest vestal gold, / And brimmed with sunlight's crystal wine." "The Butterfly" is a five-part poem in 80 lines where the butterfly's beauty is referred to as "a nameless pain" because it hints at "Beauty's frail impermanence." In contrast, "To a Yellow Pine" is a paean to the tree that "standeth here, apart, alone, / A lord of splendid solitudes, / Where man his presence rare intrudes / And to his spoiling hand known."

"Black Enchantment" is perhaps the closest Smith came during this period to pure horror. The narrator sees himself as a "silent ghost with thinnest cerement pale," wandering in the depths of a forest and coming upon what can only be the symbols of death. In the end:

> A night within the night was opened out—
> Some iron bubble of enormous dread
> From Death's abysm: Dwindled to a doubt,
> The visible live world for me was fled;
> Alone with all the immemorial dead,—
> Sharing that burden with the breathless gloom—
> I sensed the unheard intolerable tread
> Of those unnumbered legions of the tomb.

Not only death itself, but the accumulated deaths of all the entities that preceded him on this earth, constitute the "burden" (i.e., message) of the vision the narrator experiences. This is perhaps a bleaker portrayal of the evanescence of beauty, and of all life, that is stressed elsewhere with wistful poignancy rather than terror.

Smith finds in night a potent symbol for death but also (as the poem "Night" declares) a "Mistress of peace . . . who quiet brings." But "The Vampire Night" seeks to evoke the terrors of darkness in a mode of pure horror: "Lo, I seem to hark / The gabblings of the grave, where speak anights / The neighbouring dead; strange outcry of the corpse / Unhallowed by the ghoul's disturbing hand, / And mumblings out of brainless skulls."

"To Thomas Paine" consists of a pair of sonnets that are perhaps uncharacteristic of Smith in that they constitute a rare departure from the idea of "pure poetry" to which he appears to have been unconsciously gravitating. Their subject, of course, is the Anglo-American pamphleteer Thomas Paine (1737–1809), who is here praised not for his screeds on the American Revolution (*Common Sense*, 1776; *The American Crisis*, 1776–83), but for *The Age of Reason* (1794), which excoriated orthodox religion; this led to accusations that he was an atheist and worse, although in reality he was a deist who sought to purge religion of its more crudely supernatural features (especially its reliance on biblical "miracles") so as to make it more intellectually credible in an age that had made such significant strides in science and philosophy. Smith duly speaks of Paine's role in "The fading of the priests and powers of gloom." If any evidence of Smith's freethinking is needed, this is sufficient.

"The Road of Pain" and "Death" are also moralistic poems, the first pessimistic, the other finding solace in death. Interestingly, a poem in six quatrains, "To George Sterling"—one of six poems that Smith wrote over the years to his mentor, and one that uses Sterling's patented *abba* rhyme scheme (itself derived from Tennyson)—explicitly notes Sterling as a model and shows Smith as a humble follower:

> Yet though I breathe a fainter tone,
> And bring to Beauty's deathless shrine
> A lesser offering than thine,
> Whose blooms in loftier soil are grown,

*   *   *

Mayhap the note that I have sung,
    Obedient to the Muse's call,
    Is not in vain; the coronal
Of fragile flowers not voidly flung.

There is no evidence that Smith ever sent this poem to Sterling.

It must have been some of these poems of 1910–11 that inclined a teacher in Auburn, Emily Hamilton, to recommend George Sterling as someone who could help Smith become established as a poet or, at a minimum, aid in his poetic development. Smith's first letter to Sterling, written in early to mid-January 1911 and enclosing "The Butterfly" and other poems, reached the older poet in a circuitous fashion, as it had been sent to Piedmont (a city in California, near Oakland, where Sterling had lived between 1890 and 1905) and had to be forwarded to his residence in Carmel-by-the-Sea. Sterling responded on 31 January, and the relationship of these like-minded writers began at once and continued over the next fifteen years. Under Sterling's tutelage Smith not only blossomed as a poet but achieved significant early renown. Poetry would remain a vital aesthetic outlet for the remainder of his life.

Reviews

Firelight and Nightmuse: Two Poets Find Their Voices

Steven Withrow

ADAM BOLIVAR. *Told by Firelight in Timbered Halls: A Wordhord of Alliterative Verse.* [Salem, OR]: Jackanapes Press, 2025. 130 pp. $15.99 tpb. SCOTT J. COUTURIER. *Nightmuse: Poems of Speculative Darkness.* [Salem, OR]: Jackanapes Press, 2025. 110 pp. $15.99 tpb.

Rather than attempting a sprawling analysis of these two excellent new collections from Jackanapes Press, I've decided to show how three defining qualities of each writer are embodied in an exceptional piece from each book.

Told by Firelight in Timbered Halls, a book of Modern English poems adeptly composed using the Old English alliterative metrical system, includes everything that one needs to read it well. The foreword and introduction situate the poems in literary history and in Adam Bolivar's oeuvre. Equally informative are the side notes and Bolivar's brief guide to alliterative verse. Also, publisher/designer Daniel V. Sauer has created a phenomenal package that includes beautiful typography and a range of well-chosen public-domain artwork.

The Black Shepherd

The Black Shepherd   bides in darkness,
Shimmering his lantern,   shining wanly,
Making mischief   on a moonless night
For reckless fools   enraptured by the spark,
And follow it far   into the fearful moor,

> Ghostlight guided.   Godly his power,
> The Shepherd makes   a sharp judgment,
> Granting the guileless   a grim ending,
> Drowned, deathtaken   in deep water,
> But the worthy he picks   for his wayward flock,
> Leading them safely   with his light's flicker,
> A spark kindled   in the sprywitted,
> Heart heathenturned   who heeds his call.

The first of Bolivar's defining qualities is the most abstract or holistic. This is his *unflagging sincerity* about his folkloric and mythical subject matter. (It is also a trait shared by Frank Coffman, the book's foreword writer.) Bolivar is not content to be a loose translator or parodist of Old English verse; his is not an art of mere pastiche or self-reflexive antiquarianism. Instead, he is an inspired maker who clearly does his best to inhabit the spirit—and as close to the letter as our upstart tongue will allow—of the Anglo-Saxon poet or scop. Even when Bolivar is being ironic or humorous, he does so in a fashion that honors the time-tested grace of the oral tradition.

The second quality is rooted in the poet's craft and reflects Bolivar's *exacting attention* to detail and sound. I was fortunate to receive an early version of "The Black Shepherd" and to trace the careful revisions the writer made as he improved his command of Old English prosody and refined his powers of description. Compare lines four and five above, as published in *Spectral Realms* 23, to those in an earlier version:

> Wayward rovers,   bewitched by the spark,
> Follow it further   into the fearful heath,

To my ear, the revision outmatches the draft both at the level of meaning and in the sonic contours of the phrases. Case in point: in contrast with "heath," the word "moor" echoes "far" and "fear-" without introducing full rhyme where it would feel out of place. Also, in the previous line Bolivar has sharpened the alliteration with the strong rhotic consonants in "reckless" and "enraptured" compared with the slightly weaker <w> sounds in "wayward" and "bewitched" (with "wayward" reemerging in line 10 of the final version). Such are the challenges and joys of writing formal verse.

The third quality exemplified by "The Black Shepherd," and omnipresent in this fine collection as a whole, is Bolivar's *subtle mastery* of dynamic registers of speech. The second of the poem's two complete sentences moves from a sort of plain style: vivid, direct, and perfect for narrative efficiency—

> The Shepherd makes   a sharp judgment,
> Granting the guileless   a grim ending,

—to a much more indirect (I'll call it *slantwise*) style that nearly escapes simple paraphrase while still providing a memorable conclusion, intensified by the unusual and hyphenless kennings:

> A spark kindled   in the sprywitted,
> Heart heathenturned   who heeds his call.

"Heathenturned" indeed! This is poetry of a rare and high order. Do seek it out.

Nightmuse: Poems of Speculative Darkness, a satisfying mixture of medium-length and short poems that range from the macabre to the dark fantastic, is a confident step forward for Scott Couturier since his first collection, *I Awaken in October: Poems of Folk Horror and Halloween,* appeared in 2022. This new book is leaner and more focused than the first, and its strongest pieces—blendings of seductive narrative with high-voltage description—are made for reading aloud. And *Nightmuse* also features one of Dan Sauer's most stunning covers.

Nightmare

> Some scuttling thing scratching behind the walls—
> rat or bird trapped there, it always comes from
> that same corner, setting my flesh to crawl.
> They call sanity a treasure sans sum,
> madness making even emperors poor:
> so I must wonder what is scratching there,
> vermin or gust, ghost or gremlin, implore
> myself for patience at each sudden scare.
> *Scritch, scratch, scritch* it sounds, at odd hours of night,
> bat or bitumen-black demon, loose board
> budged by unseasonable winds—my fright
> grows as the scrabbling swells into a horde.

*   *   *

> What will burst from that corner?—angles meet
> whence waxes the scuffling of legion feet.

The first of Couturier's defining qualities is his assured *theatrical presence*. "Nightmare," a Shakespearean sonnet first published in *parABnormal Magazine* in 2020, is structured for an intense vocal performance. While this poem never quite attains a secure iambic pentameter base, falling more often into a four-beat accentual line, this is compensated for by the many skillful enjambments that allow the sentences to stretch and twist over the lines with a nervous energy that merges with the poem's eerie subject. The hanging end-line pauses after "implore," "loose board," and "my fright" are especially nice touches.

The second quality builds more comprehensively on that stretching and twisting of meaning. This is Couturier's fondness and gift for *energized excess*. Some of the longer poems in *Nightmuse* do suffer a bit from an excess of explication, a surfeit of signification even, and they might have been improved by some judicious tightening. But energized excess is a positive trait.

If placed on a spectrum across all weird verse that runs from minimalist to maximalist, Couturier's work would generally lean more toward overstatement than ellipsis. However, he is capable of penning highly effective rhapsodic moments such as in the closing couplet of "Nightmare" and in these more delicately effusive lines:

> vermin or gust, ghost or gremlin, implore
> myself for patience at each sudden scare.

The third defining quality is more difficult to name or elucidate fully, but it can be demonstrated with a single example from the sonnet:

> bat or bitumen-black demon, loose board
> budged by unseasonable winds

For lack of a better term, I will call this an instance of Couturier's heightened *aural sensitivity*. Simply put, he has a great ear for alliteration (those b's and d's!) and for the play of long and short vowels, which is poetry at the particle level. How "bat" morphs into "bitumen-black" is thrilling to me, and it brought to mind the word-music of Ray Bradbury or Ramsey Campbell. While Couturier is not always writing at this peak of intensity in *Nightmuse*, he does so often enough that I will definitely be revisiting its pages.

Lyrics and Shanties

S. T. Joshi

JOHN SHIRLEY. *Ghost Confessions*. [Salem, OR]: Jackanapes Press, 2025. 103 pp. $12.99 tpb.

It might seem counter-intuitive to think of John Shirley–author of *Wetbones* and other over-the-top horror novels–as a sensitive and thought-provoking weird poet; but readers of *Spectral Realms* know better. And let us recall that Shirley has also written song lyrics for such bands as Blue Öyster Cult–which, whatever one may think of their musical settings, are definitely poetry of a grim and powerful sort.

This new poetry collection–Shirley's second, following *The Voice of the Burning House* (2021)–embodies all those elements that make his verse memorable. In form, we have a wide diversity ranging from tightly written sonnets ("Three Sonnets of the Weird") to narrative poems ("And Then He Died") to pensive quatrains ("Houses as Boxes of Drama") to philosophical verse ("Gaia's Reckoning"), where Gaia (the Earth) condemns its purportedly supreme inhabitants: "My kaleidoscope will whirl in glory / And up will rise a newborn story: / Nature returns to sanity– / *And I won't bring back humanity.*" We even have a sea shanty ("The Thing That Broke Johansen") manifestly elaborating upon the character of that name in Lovecraft's "The Call of Cthulhu" ("Then from the depths of oozing R'lyeh / Reared a thing taller than the tallest tree").

"All the Kids Are Trippin'" is one of several poems that are explicitly identified as a (song) "lyric"–and its compact account of demoralized young people ("All the kids are trippin' / Flailing for their trail / Lost children at a carnival / flap like frightened quail") cries out for musical adaptation by a suitable rock band.

In his introduction Shirley speaks a bit defensively about retaining the use of rhyme and meter, rightly pointing out that such weird poets as Ann K. Schwader, Wade German, and K. A. Opperman have achieved greatness precisely through such use—to say nothing of their own spectral imaginations. But Shirley is careful to note that he has also drawn inspiration from those poets who didn't always adhere to strict form, ranging from Carl Sandburg to the Beat poets. But it was Lovecraft and Clark Ashton Smith whom Shirley acknowledges as his chief models in weird poetry. It hardly needs to be stated that he merely draws inspiration from these and other poets in fashioning poetry that, in its brooding melancholy, is very much his own.

This book is one more sterling production from Jackanapes Press, whose ever-growing line of weird poetry is becoming more impressive by the day. Under the leadership of its publisher, Daniel V. Sauer, this book—like all its predecessors and, no doubt, its successors—is meticulously designed, presenting the poems in a clear and elegant type and surrounding them with tasteful but effective illustrations that augment their effect. If the renaissance of weird poetry that has been underway for several decades is to continue, it will owe a considerable debt of gratitude to Jackanapes Press.

Notes on Contributors

Dmitri Akers is a warrior-poet and weird practitioner living in Kaurna country (Adelaide, South Australia). His poetry has bewitched *Spectral Realms* ever since "The Whale Road" first appeared in the 18th issue (Winter 2023). He has amassed five horror short stories; these terrible spectres haunt *Penumbra, Spawn II, Skull & Laurel,* and *The Deadlands.* He is currently an undergraduate student at the Photography Studies College in Narrm (Melbourne, Victoria).

Eli Alemán is a Puerto Rican scientist and speculative poet whose work explores the intersection of biology, myth, and the macabre. Raised by the Caribbean Sea, she now draws inspiration from colder northern shores. She brings a scientific eye to the supernatural, with poetry in *Eye to the Telescope* and *Spectral Realms.* Her debut collection, *Neon Lights and Plane Tickets,* received a 2024 Elgin Award nomination.

David Barker has been writing supernatural fiction and poetry since the 1980s. His latest book is *12 Foot Skeleton Poems.* David's work has appeared in many magazines and anthologies, including *Fungi, Cyäegha, Weird Fiction Review, The Audient Void, Nightmare's Realm, Forbidden Knowledge, Spectral Realms, The Art Mephitic, A Walk in a Darker Wood, A Walk in a City of Shadows, For the Outsider: Poems Inspired by H. P. Lovecraft,* and *Weird Fiction Quarterly.*

F. J. Bergmann writes poetry and speculative fiction, sometimes horribly, and is the poetry editor of *Mobius: The Journal of Social Change.* She has won three Rhysling Awards, two Elgin Awards for chapbooks, is a past editor of *Star*Line,* and is SFPA's most recent Grand Master. She likes to ride horses. She is pretty sure she'd like to ride unicorns, if only they'd cooperate.

Adam Bolivar is a formal poet of folkloric fantasy, a weird fiction writer, and a playwright for marionettes, with a particular interest in alliterative verse, balladry, and "Jack" tales. He is the author of several books, including *The Ettinfell of Beacon Hill* (Jackanapes Press, 2021), *Ballads for* the *Witching Hour* (Hippocampus Press, 2022), and *Told by Firelight in Timbered Halls* (Jackanapes Press, 2025). A native of Boston, he now resides in Portland, Oregon.

Pixie Bruner is a writer, editor, and cancer survivor. She lives in Atlanta with her doppelgänger and their deranged cats. Editor of *Memento Mori Ink Magazine*'s "Morsus Vitae," her Elgin Award–nominated book *The Body as Haunted* was published by Authortunities Press in 2024. Her words are in/forthcoming from *Space & Time, Hotel Macabre Vol. 1* (Crystal Lake Publishing), *Amazing Stories, Star*Line, Weird Fiction Quarterly, Abyss & Apex, Penumbric,* Angry Gable Press, and many more. She wrote for White Wolf Gaming Studio. She is a 2024 SFPA Pushcart Prize nominee and 2025 Rhysling Award Chair.

Jason Ray Carney is a Senior Lecturer in the Department of English at Christopher Newport University. He is the author of *Weird Tales of Modernity: The Ephemerality of the Ordinary in the Stories of Robert E. Howard, Clark Ashton Smith, and H. P. Lovecraft* (McFarland, 2019). His reviews and essays have appeared in the *Los Angeles Review of Books, The Washington Independent Review of Books, Black Gate,* and others. He is the Managing Editor of Spiral Tower Press.

Scott J. Couturier is a Rhysling Award–nominated poet and prose writer of the weird, liminal, and darkly fantastic. His work has appeared in numerous venues, including *The Audient Void, Spectral Realms, Tales from the Magician's Skull, Space and Time, Cosmic Horror Monthly,* and *Weirdbook.* His collection of weird fiction, *The Box,* is available from Hybrid Sequence Media, while his collection of autumnal and folk horror verse, *I Awaken in October,* is available from Jackanapes Press.

A. J. Dalton is a UK-based writer. He has published the *Empire of the Saviours* trilogy with Gollancz Orion, *The Satanic in Science Fiction and Fantasy* with Luna Press, the poetry collection *Dark Woods Rising* with Starship Sloane, and other works. He lives with his monstrously oppressive cat named Cleopatra.

Nicholas De Marino is analog head swapper, furniture saboteur, and escaped content farm workhorse. He has several writing credits in bathroom stalls and a hopelessly indulgent column in *foofaraw*. ¡Viva SFPA and Codex!

Christian Dickinson is an Assistant Professor of English Literature at Faulkner University. His professional interests include the Victorian novel, poetry, and the role of religion in nineteenth-century English literary life and culture. In addition to his work in *Spectral Realms*, Dickinson's poetry has appeared in *ParABnormal*, *The Mythic Circle*, and *Illumen*. He has also published two books of religious poetry based on the Psalms, available now from Orison Publishers.

Kendall Evans's poems have appeared in *Asimov's*, *Dreams & Nightmares*, *Star*Line*, *Analog*, *Spectral Realms*, *Weird Tales*, and many other periodicals and anthologies. He is also the author of the novels *The Rings of Ganymede* and *Tales of the Chinese Pirate Princess Ching Shih*.

Wade German's most recent full-length poetry collection is *Psalms and Sorceries* (Hippocampus Press, 2022). His first collection, *Dreams from a Black Nebula*, is also available from Hippocampus Press. Other titles include several slim volumes of his selected poems with Portuguese translation, most recently the chapbook *Noctivagations* (Raphus Press, 2024).

Alper Ghuchlu is a lifelong fan of science fiction, fantasy, and horror now writing stories of his own, some of which have been published in *Star*Line*, *Daikaijuzine*, *Dreams and Nightmares*, *Night to Dawn*, *Scifaikuest*, various anthologies, and elsewhere.

Maxwell I. Gold is a Jewish-American multiple award-nominated author who writes prose poetry and short stories in cosmic horror and weird fiction with half a decade of writing experience. He is a five-time Rhysling Award nominee and two-time Pushcart Award nominee.

Norbert Góra is a thirty-five-year-old poet and writer from Poland. He is the author of more than 130 poems published in many anthologies and magazines around the world. He has also written three dark poetry books in English—*A Globe Bathed in Horror*, *Darkness in the End*, and *There Must Be Something Between Dark and Light* (a collection of haikus)—and one short story collection of horror, *Brutality*. He is inspired by both the light and the murkiness.

Joshua Green is an author of weird fiction, fantasy, and science fiction. His work has appeared or is forthcoming in *British Fantasy Society: Horizons*, *Strange Aeon*, *Spectral Realms*, *Penumbra*, *Calliope Interactive*, and elsewhere. He has three wonderful children and a miniature Australian shepherd named Juni.

Jay Hardy is a poet and artist living in southern Louisiana. He is a lifelong fan of horror, dark fiction and science fiction. He has self-published several poetry collections including *Living Longmire*, *Always Eleven*, *Cairo Cats*, and *My Mommy Hates Halloween*. His weird poetry is published in *Spectral Realms*, *Lovecraftiana*, *View from Atlantis*, *Ellery Queen's Mystery Magazine*, and *Hyborian Gazette*.

S. T. Joshi is the editor of *Spectral Realms* and author of the forthcoming biography *The Star-Treader: A Life of Clark Ashton Smith* (Hippocampus Press), from which the essay included here is an extract.

With a background in the arts (non-dark), customer service and administration, travel, and tourism, and education, **Janice Klain** has plenty of experiences to draw from as she journeys through the world of the written word.

David C. Kopaska-Merkel won the 2006 Rhysling Award for best long poem (for a collaboration with Kendall Evans), and edits *Dreams & Nightmares* magazine. He has edited *Star*Line*, an issue of *Eye to the Telescope*, and several Rhysling anthologies. His poems have been published in *Analog*, *Asimov's*, *Strange Horizons*, and elsewhere. *Some Disassembly Required*, a collection of dark speculative poetry, won the 2023 Elgin Award. His latest collection, *Unwholesome Guests*, was published in 2024 by Weird House.

Lori R. Lopez is a quirky author, illustrator, poet, and songwriter who likes to wear hats. Her Gothic-toned and extensive poetry collection *Darkverse: The Shadow Hours* was nominated for the 2018 Elgin Award, while individual poems have been nominated for Rhysling Awards.

Stories and verse appear in numerous publications. Other titles include *The Dark Mister Snark, Leery Lane, Odds & Ends, The room at the end of the hall, Cryptic Consequences,* and *An Ill Wind Blows.*

Simon MacCulloch lives in London and writes poetry for a variety of print and online journals. He has garnered numerous rejections, not only for his poems but also for his biographical note and his photograph. When he is not writing, he enjoys pondering bitterly on this.

David McLachlan lives and works in Northern California, a place that inspires much of his fiction and poetry. He has degrees in mathematics and economics and an MFA in Creative Writing from Warren Wilson College. His stories and poems have been published or are forthcoming in numerous magazines and anthologies.

Ngo Binh Anh Khoa is a teacher of English in Ho Chi Minh City, Vietnam. In his free time he enjoys daydreaming, reading, and occasionally writing poetry for personal entertainment. His speculative poems have appeared in NewMyths.com, *Heroic Fantasy Quarterly, The Audient Void,* and other venues.

Of **Manuel Pérez-Campos**'s poems, one garnered a special appearance that assumed the lead position in *Lovecraft Annual* No. 15, completely unprecedented because this periodical is otherwise not a forum for verse; another poem appeared in *For the Outsider: Poems Inspired by H. P. Lovecraft,* edited by S.T. Joshi. His poems have been seen mostly in prior issues of *Spectral Realms.* He lives in Bayamón, Puerto Rico.

Flavia Pierret is a writer and medical student from Cuba. Her poetry bridges the pathos of Romanticism with the visionary imagery of Spanish mysticism, exploring the thin membrane between the sacred and the profane. This is her first appearance in *Spectral Realms.*

Michael Potts is the author of three novels: *End of Summer, Unpardonable Sin,* and *Obedience,* all published by WordCrafts Press. He also has published three volumes of poetry: *From Field to Thicket* (winner, 2006 Mary Belle Campbell Poetry Book Award, North Carolina Writers Network), *Hiding from the Reaper and Other Horror Poems,* and *Slipknot and*

Other Dark Poems. He serves as Professor of Philosophy, Methodist University, Fayetteville, North Carolina.

Geoffrey Reiter is Associate Professor and Coordinator of Literature at Lancaster Bible College. He is also an associate editor at the website *Christ and Pop Culture*, where he frequently writes about weird horror and dark fantasy. As a scholar of weird fiction, Reiter has published academic articles on such authors as Arthur Machen, Bram Stoker, Clark Ashton Smith, and William Peter Blatty. His poetry has previously appeared in *Spectral Realms* and *Star*Line*. His fiction is collected in *The Lime Kiln and Other Enchanted Spaces* (Hippocampus Press, 2025).

Silvatiicus Riddle is a four-time Rhysling-nominated dark fantasy/ speculative fiction writer and poet haunting the bones of an old amusement park on the edge of New York City. His work has appeared or is forthcoming in *Strange Horizons, Apex Magazine, Enchanted Living, Eternal Haunted Summer, Spectral Realms,* and *Creepy Podcast*, among others. He combats despair and entropy with his newsletter, *The Goblin's Reliquary*.

Michael Rollins lives and works in Barrow in Furness, Cumbria, England, as an English teacher and artist. He writes poetry and short stories, some of which have been published in collections; his personal favorite is *Bones and Feathers*, a volume of poetry written with an Indian poet, Preeti Rana.

Allan Rozinski is a writer of speculative fiction and poetry who has had poetry published in *Spectral Realms, Weirdbook, Horror Writers Association Poetry Showcase, The Rhysling Anthology, Eternal Haunted, Summer, Star*Line*, and other publications.

Ann K. Schwader lives and writes in Colorado. Her newest collection, *Unquiet Stars*, is now out from Weird House Press. Two of her earlier collections, *Wild Hunt of the Stars* (Sam's Dot, 2010) and *Dark Energies* (P'rea Press, 2015), were Bram Stoker Award finalists. In 2018, she received the Science Fiction and Fantasy Poetry Association's Grand Master Award. She is also a two-time Rhysling Award winner.

Darrell Schweitzer has been publishing weird or fantastic poetry for decades. His two previous collections of (mostly weird) verse are *Groping toward the Light* (2000) and *Ghosts of Past and Future* (2008). Hippocampus Press issued a new volume of previously uncollected and selected poems, *Dancing Before Azathoth*, in 2025. His most recent story collection is *The Children of Chorazin* (Hippocampus Press, 2023) and his most recent anthology is *Weird Tales: The Best of the 1920s* (Centipede Press, 2025).

John Shirley won the Bram Stoker Award for his book *Black Butterflies: A Flock on the Dark Side*. His first poetry collection, *The Voice of the Burning House,* has been nominated for the Elgin Award for poetry.

Oliver Smith is an artist and writer from Cheltenham, Gloucestershire, UK. His poetry has appeared in *Dreams & Nightmares, Eye to the Telescope, Illumen, Mirror Dance, Rivet, Spectral Realms, Star*Line,* and *Weirdbook.* His collection of stories, *Stars Beneath the Ships,* was published by Ex Occidente Press in 2017, and many of his previously anthologized stories and poems are collected in *Basilisk Soup and Other Fantasies.* Smith is studying for a Ph.D. in Creative Writing.

Jay Sturner is an award-winning poet, fiction writer, and naturalist from the Chicago suburbs. He is the author of several books of poetry and a collection of short stories. His writing has appeared in such publications as the *Magazine of Fantasy & Science Fiction, Space & Time, Not One of Us, Star*Line,* and *Spectral Realms.*

Arukoya Tomais was born in Japan. Her father was of Chinese descent and moved to Japan due to political prejudice, fearing he would be jailed if he did not abandon his home country. Her mother is an American who traveled to Japan as a journalist and met Arukoya's father. She moved to the U.S. in January 2024, where she met the poet Kendall Evans at a Steampunk convention in San Diego. He encouraged her to begin submitting her work, and she has sold poems to both *Star*Line* and *Dreams & Nightmares.*

DJ Tyrer is the person behind Atlantean Publishing and has been published in *The Rhysling Anthology 2016,* issues of *Cyaegha, The Horrorzine, Scifaikuest, Sirens Call, Star*Line, Tigershark,* and *The Yellow*

Zine. SuperTrump and *A Wuhan Whodunnit* are available to download from the Atlantean Publishing website. The collection *Madness Rides the Star-Wind* is published by Island of Wak-Wak.

Yuliia Vereta is a Polish writer of Ukrainian origin who is now living her third life in Katowice, where she works as a translator. Her speculative works have been published in print and online, among others in *Star*Line*, *Dreams and Nightmares*, *Asimov's Science Fiction*, *Leading Edge*, *Penumbric*, *Kaleidotrope*, and *ParSec*. She is a 2022 Best of the Net nominee.

Jacqueline West's poetry has appeared in *Pyre Magazine*, *Star*Line*, *Abyss & Apex*, and *Strange Horizons*, and has received five Rhysling nominations, three Pushcart nominations, and a Dorothy Sargent Rosenberg Prize. Her books for young readers include the *New York Times* bestselling dark fantasy series *The Books of Elsewhere* and the young adult horror novel *Last Things*.

Andrew White lives in the mountains of North Carolina, where he jots down a poem from time to time. He derives inspiration from the mystical, the mythological, and all things Gothic/Lovecraftian. Andrew loves nature, his family, and black metal. A handful of his poems have been published, mostly in *Spectral Realms*.

Steven Withrow has written three chapbooks—*The Sun Ships*, *The Bedlam Philharmonic*, and *The Nothing Box*—and a collaborative collection, *The Exorcised Lyric* (with Frank Coffman). His speculative and dark fantasy poems have appeared in *Asimov's*, *Spectral Realms*, *Space & Time*, and *Dreams & Nightmares*. His work was nominated for the Rhysling and Elgin Awards, and he wrote the libretto for a chamber opera based on a classic English ghost story. He lives on Cape Cod.

Andrew Paul Wood is a cultural historian, art critic, essayist, translator, and editor based in New Zealand. He serves as Art and Comics Editor at *takahē* magazine and contributes regularly to publications in New Zealand, Australia, the United Kingdom, and the US, and several of his essays on H. P. Lovecraft can be found in the *Lovecraft Annual*. He has written a history of occultism in New Zealand, *Shadow Worlds* (Massey University Press, 2023).

Lee Clark Zumpe, an entertainment editor with Tampa Bay Newspapers, earned his bachelor's degree in English at the University of South Florida. He began writing poetry and fiction in the early 1990s. His work has regularly appeared in a variety of literary journals and genre magazines over the last few decades.

www.ingramcontent.com/pod-product-compliance
Lightning Source LLC
Chambersburg PA
CBHW060806050426
42449CB00008B/1560